W9-CRQ-874

NTC/Contemporary Publishing Group

Library of Congress Cataloging-in-Publication Data is on file at the United States Library of Congress

Published by NTC Publishing Group
An imprint of NTC/Contemporary Publishing Group
Copyright © 2000 Brian Senior
4255 West Touhy Avenue, Lincolnwood (Chicago)
Illinois 60646- 1975 U.S.A.

Printed in Singapore
International Standard Book Number:
0-8442-2226-7

contents

foreword

Bridge is a game enjoyed by many millions of players all over the world.

In these days of rising commercial pressures, increasing leisure and greater longevity, bridge has the potential to break down social and ethnic barriers and to keep the wheels of the brain turning in both the old and the young. Apart from that, bridge at whatever level is a very inexpensive game, all you need to play is a flat surface that the four players can sit round with a pack of cards and, of course, an understanding as to how to play the game.

It is for these reasons that I am particularly pleased to welcome the 'How to Play Bridge' series which has been specially designed to make the game easy to follow for beginners, no matter what their age. I believe that you will find the whole series well presented and particularly easy to read.

Bobby Wolff
Dallas, Texas
March 1997

introduction

If your opponents could be relied upon to keep quiet during the auction, then all the rules and guidelines for constructive bidding which you have so painstakingly learned would allow you to reach the correct contract most of the time and a sensible one almost always. Alas, your opponents will not keep quiet. Frequently, they will have opened the bidding before you get a chance to do so and now many of your rules will no longer be appropriate to the different situation in which you find yourself.

Once an opponent opens the bidding you need a new set of rules and guidelines to ally to your judgement. For example, you pick up a hand with which you would have opened 1♣ or 1♦ and. before you get a chance to speak, your right-hand-opponent (RHO) opens 1♥. What are you to do?

This is one reason why you need to follow different rules. Another is that the very fact that an opponent has guaranteed a reasonable hand by bidding makes it that little bit more dangerous for you to bid. Finally, the odds have improved that the hand will eventually be played by the opposition. You may wish to make a bid which will make it difficult for your opponents to explore the hand properly and therefore harder to reach their best contract, or you may wish to make a bid which will help to get partner off to the best opening lead for your side.

There are a range of different defensive (i.e. bids made after an opponent has opened) bids available to you but none,mean exactly the same as they would have done had you been allowed to open the bidding.

You can overcall, which means that you bid a new suit or 1NT; you can make a jump overcall in either a suit or in no trump, which means exactly what it sounds like; you can make a double or even bigger jump overcall; and there are two new options which are only available because an opponent has bid. These last two possibilities are to cuebid the opponents' suit, and to make a takeout double.

We will look at all of these options in turn; not only what they mean and what type of hand would choose each option but how to decide which option to choose, how to respond when it is partner who bids over an enemy opening bid, and how to continue the auction from that point. By the end of the book you may be exhausted by all the ground we have covered but your basic defensive bidding should be in pretty good shape.

the opponents overcall one of a suit

the simple overcall

If you bid a new suit over an opponent's opening bid you are making what is known as an overcall. An overcall at the one-level promises a reasonable five card or longer suit and around 8-15 HCP. To overcall at the two-level, which involves your side in contracting to make an extra trick, requires a little more strength, just as you might expect. The maximum for a two-level overcall is still about 15 HCP but the minimum is nearer to 11 HCP, in other words a hand including a decent five card or longer suit and which would have opened the bidding at the one-level had it had the opportunity to do so.

There are two major changes from opening the bidding. The first is that you must hold a reasonable five card suit whatever the suit you bid, while you can open one of a major on any five card suit, however weak, and one of a minor with three cards. This is really a matter of safety. If you overcall on a scrappy four-card suit and find left-hand-opponent (LHO) with both length and strength in the suit you could find yourself in big trouble, doubled and going for a large penalty.

The other change is that you are allowed to overcall at the one-level on hands with insufficient high-card strength to have opened the bidding. This is provided that you have a reasonable suit and the benefits of coming into the bidding on these hands in the 8-11 HCP range are firstly to suggest a safe opening lead to partner and secondly to try to disrupt the flow of information between your opponents. Imagine, for example, how much more difficult it will be for them if you overcall 1 ♠ and partner can find a quiet raise to 2 ♠ than if you both remain silent. Without doing anything dramatic you have taken away a significant amount of bidding space and if your opponents should be playing the hand it will be that much more difficult for them to reach the best contract.

These are typical minimum overcalls at the one-
and two-levels respectively when RHO opens 1♥.

(a)   ♠   KJ1087   (b)   ♠   A8
          ♥   A4   ♥   965
          ♦   863   ♦   AQJ84
          ♣   1095   ♣   J54

In fact, vulnerable you might prefer to strengthen
the second hand slightly. After all, you are
contracting to make eight tricks and there is no
guarantee that partner will be able to help much.

The following hands would not be suitable for an
overcall.

(c)   ♠   J8643   (d)   ♠   Q86
          ♥   Q42   ♥   Q54
          ♦   AJ   ♦   Q8765
          ♣   1097   ♣   AQ

Both have the same length of main suit as the
previous examples and the same overall number of
HCP but the main suits are very weak. While you
might occasionally overcall with a weak suit,
particularly at the one-level, when holding a better
hand, there is little benefit and plenty of risk
attached to doing so with a minimum in terms of
high cards. You have no reason to point partner
towards a lead of such a poor suit. These are
precisely the types of suit which leave open the
possibility that LHO will have length and strength
in your suit and play for a penalty.

I have said that the top end of the range for a
simple overcall is around 15 HCP. We will see
later what to do with stronger hands.

responding to an overcall

When partner overcalls you may respond with very
little if you have support for his suit, and because
he has promised at least five cards you can
support him with three, just as when facing a
1 ♥ / ♠ opening. We will come back to raising
partner in a moment.

Lacking support for partner, you should usually
pass unless you have at least nine or ten HCP.
There is little prospect of game when you have no
fit and know there cannot be 25 HCP between the
two hands. Note that the fact that partner is limited
to 15 HCP means that there is no need to scrape
up a response in the way that you sometimes do
when he opens the bidding just to give him a
second chance to speak with a strong hand. Even
if you dislike partner's suit quite strongly, it is
generally best to pass if weak. There is no rescue
of an overcall; if you respond partner is entitled to
expect you to have a reasonable hand.

So after the start:

West	North	East	South
1 ♣	1 ♥	Pass	?

South Holds:

- ♠ A86
- ♥ 7
- ♦ KJ753
- ♣ 9542

Had partner opened 1 ♥, you would have responded 1NT. Here, you should just pass. You should not bid no trump with no stopper in a suit bid by the opposition and are not strong enough to bid a new suit at the two-level. As game is not likely, just pass and hope that partner can make 1 ♥ if LHO also passes.

A new suit response to an overcall should usually be a five card or longer suit, though you might bid a new four card suit at the one-level on occasions. While not everybody plays that way, the simplest approach is to play that a change of suit is forcing for one round, just as opposite an opening bid. That way, when you hold a good hand you can explore it properly without having to worry about partner passing at an inconvenient moment.

A sensible approach which allows you to utilise the rules of bidding with which you are already familiar is to say that a new suit from responder is always forcing while a reverse or jump by the overcaller is also strong but a repeat of his first suit or a new suit below the next level of his first suit is weaker and can be passed. So:

(a)	West	North	East	South
	1♣	1♥	Pass	2♦
	Pass	2♥	Pass	2♠

2♦ is forcing for one round, showing at least the strength to have responded 2♦ to a 1♥ opening bid; 2♥ is consistent with a minimum overcall and is passable; 2♠ is a new suit from responder and so forcing.

(b)	West	North	East	South
	1♦	1♠	Pass	2♣
	Pass	?		

2♣ is a one-round force. If North rebids 2♥, 2♠ or 3♣, South is allowed to pass. All are consistent with a minimum overcall. A 2NT rebid is also passable, though it does show extra values, say about 12 HCP plus a sure diamond stopper, but it denies the ability to jump to 3NT, as would a 14-15 point hand. If North wants to force he jumps to 3♥, 3♠ or 4♣.

There is one other possibility for the overcaller who has a strong hand. That is to cuebid the opponents' suit. The assumption is that once an opponent has bid a suit it is unlikely that the other side will want to play with that suit as trumps.

There are certain situations in which that is not quite true but it is not a bad rule to have at this stage in your bridge careers.

That being the case, you would never want to bid the opponents' suit in a natural sense. A very useful alternative is to play that a bid of a suit already shown by an opponent is completely artificial. We will come across this again and the precise meaning of the bid will vary according to the situation, but here the overcaller might bid the opponents' suit to show a strong hand, near maximum for the initial overcall, but with no clear descriptive bid he can make at this point. For example:

West	North	East	South
1 ♦	1 ♠	Pass	2 ♣
Pass	?		

North Holds:

- ♠ AQ1086
- ♥ AK4
- ♦ 875
- ♣ Q7

North has 15 HCP, a complete maximum for his 1 ♠ call, and expects that game should be on after South's two-over-one response. Yet what can he bid? He cannot support clubs with a doubleton, cannot bid a new suit, and has already shown five spades so has nothing extra to show there. He would like to bid no trump, which would describe his distribution well, but unfortunately has no diamond stopper.

Perhaps you think that doesn't matter? What suit do you think the opposition are likely to lead if you play in no trump? It is most likely to be the one they have bid, isn't it? You may have 28 HCP between you but this will not help you to make 3NT if the opposition take the first five or six tricks. It is a good rule that, once your opponents have bid a suit, the first member of your side to bid no trump must have at least one stopper in the suit. That way you can be sure of gaining the lead at least once to take your own tricks before they can cash all of theirs.

Anyway, to go back to the example above; a 2♦ cuebid, showing a good hand and asking partner to describe his hand further, is the ideal solution to North's problem. Perhaps partner has the required diamond stopper and can bid no trumps.

When partner overcalls and you have 9+ HCP, no real support for his suit nor a good suit of your own but a sure stopper in the opponents' suit, you may respond in no trump. All no trump bids are constructive so in response to a one-level overcall 1NT shows about 9-11 HCP, 2NT 12-14 and 3NT 15+. If the overcall was at the two-level you need less because partner has promised more. You would bid 2NT on 10-12 or perhaps nine with a fitting honor to help run partner's long suit, and 3NT with 13+ HCP.

raising partner

I promised that we would return to the situation where responder has support for partner's overcall. There are two possible schemes here.

The simple scheme which is taught to beginners is that a simple raise shows about 6-10 points, a jump raise (1 ♥ – 3 ♥) 11-13, and a raise to game at least 14. A similar scheme might apply facing a two-level overcall but bear in mind that 3NT is often easier to make than five of a minor even when you have a trump fit so strong responding hands might start by cuebidding the opponents' suit to see if partner can bid no trump.

The slightly more complex scheme which, sometimes in a modified form, is used by most tournament players, utilises the cuebid of the opponents' suit to differentiate between strong and weak raises of the overcaller's suit. Traditionally, a cuebid by the overcaller's partner used to show any game-forcing hand but, given that you play a change of suit as forcing, there is really no need for that. Instead, play a cuebid in this situation as being specifically a constructive raise of partner's suit. So, for example:

West	North	East	South
1 ♦	1 ♠	Pass	?

(a)
- ♠ Q85
- ♥ A42
- ♦ 7543
- ♣ 1085

Bid 2♠, not so much because you expect to make game opposite a simple overcall, though that is still possible if partner has a distributional hand, but because if your side has a fit then so will have your opponents. They are much more likely to find their fit if you pass over 1♠ than if you raise immediately to 2♠.

(b)
- ♠ Q108
- ♥ A42
- ♦ J63
- ♣ K1097

Bid 2 ♦, initially merely promising a good raise to 2♠. This time game is much more likely and you want to encourage partner to bid on with a suitable hand.

(c)
- ♠ K1086
- ♥ A4
- ♦ 72
- ♣ J10986

Bid 3♠, invitative but at least semi-pre-emptive.

Now that you have a nine-card fit it is even more
certain that your opponents will also have a viable
trump suit elsewhere. As you are relatively low in
high cards the hand may still belong to your
opponents. A jump to 3♠ will make it very difficult
for them to get together and is safe so long as
partner is aware of the type of hand you promise.

(d)
        ♠ Q1086
        ♥ AK
        ♦ 743
        ♣ A1098

Bid 2♦, initially promising a sound raise to 2♠
but, if partner makes a weak rebid, call 3♠ next
time, showing that you had a strong game
invitation.

If you are the overcaller and hear partner cuebid in
this way – it is called an Unassuming Cuebid, by
the way, to distinguish it from the old-fashioned
general game-force – you know immediately that
he has support for your suit. With a minimum
overcall you would just repeat your suit as cheaply
as possible. If, however, you thought that game
might be on facing a good raise to 2♠ (he will bid
again anyway with a good raise to 3♠), you would
bid more strongly. Any bid other than a repeat of
your first suit would be a try for game, so:

West	North	East	South
1♣	1♥	Pass	2♣
Pass	?		

(a)
- ♠ K85
- ♥ AQ1076
- ♦ J63
- ♣ 74

Bid 2 ♥. Opposite a good raise to 2 ♥ there is no prospect of game.

(b)
- ♠ J5
- ♥ AQ1064
- ♦ AQ64
- ♣ 92

Bid 2 ♦. This is rather like a game try of 3 ♦ after partner has raised your 1 ♥ opening to 2 ♥, asking for help in diamonds and is much more helpful than, say, an invitational jump to 3 ♥. You would like to be in game opposite the two red kings plus an ace or some other combinations so are too strong not to invite game.

(c)
- ♠ A864
- ♥ KQ975
- ♦ 85
- ♣ 64

Bid 2 ♥. You have a second suit but your hand is too weak to consider game and even 3 ♥ may be too high so you must just repeat your suit.

(d)
- ♠ K53
- ♥ AQ985
- ♦ J8
- ♣ KJ2

Bid 2NT. This shows a near-maximum overcall, a
fairly balanced hand and, most importantly, at least
one sure stopper in the opponents' suit.

the 1NT overcall

Good news! If you are already thinking that
defensive bidding is complicated with a lot of new
rules to learn then you will be pleased to hear that
a 1NT overcall is almost identical to a 1NT
opening bid.

The 1NT overcall still shows a balanced
hand with 16-18 points. Occasionally
you might stretch a 15-point hand and
open 1NT if you have well-placed
honors in the suit opened on
your right. For example, KJx
is worth more than four
points when RHO has
shown length and
probably strength in a
suit.Otherwise, the only
change is that you must
have a definite stopper in the
suit bid on your right.

There is no reason to alter your
system of responses from those you use facing an
opening 1NT. If you usually play Stayman 2♣,
weak takeouts at the two-level and strong jumps,
continue to do so. After all, partner has shown

virtually the same handtype as if he had opened so you will have similar problems to overcome.

the jump overcall

There are four different types of jump overcall in use. Traditionally, a jump overcall in a new suit, e.g. 1 ♥ − 2♠/3♣, showed a strong hand, 16+ HCP and a good six card suit, and the only question was whether to play it as strong but non-forcing or strong and forcing for one round. Many people still play that way, particularly at rubber bridge.

Strong jump overcalls are all very well and are quite good for constructive bidding. Unfortunately, they come up only rarely and do nothing to make life difficult for the opposition. Tournament players came up with two different approaches, first the intermediate jump overcall and second the weak jump overcall.

An intermediate jump overcall shows a good six card suit and sound opening bid values − in the region of 12-15 HCP. Again, you will come across people who bid this way and, from the point of view solely of your own constructive bidding, this is perhaps the best approach to take, taking care as it does of hands which are a little good to just make a simple overcall then pass but which are barely worth an overcall followed by a second bid.

If you decide to play intermediate jump overcalls,

raise in the same way as opposite a simple overcall. In other words, a direct raise is not all that strong while genuine invitational hands cuebid the opponents' suit. A bid of a new suit is forcing and no trump bids are natural and constructive.

The modern trend, particularly in the tournament game, is to play weak jump overcalls. The easiest way to define a weak jump overcall is as a hand which would have opened with the same bid as dealer at the prevailing vulnerability. So a jump overcall of 2♦ /♥ /♠ shows a hand which would have opened a weak two bid, while a 3♣/♦ /♥ /♠ overcall is a hand that would have opened with a pre-emptive three-bid. Just as when opening the bidding, there will be some hands which are worth the pre-empt non-vulnerable but not if vulnerable. Typical weak jump overcalls are:

West	North	East	South
1♥	?		

(a)
        ♠ KQ10864
        ♥ 98
        ♦ 1094
        ♣ Q8

A classic 2♠ call at any vulnerability.

(b)
        ♠ A3
        ♥ 5
        ♦ KJ109753
        ♣ 643

Again, well worth 3 ♦, whatever the vulnerability.

(c) ♠ QJ2
     ♥ 74
     ♦ QJ106432
     ♣ 9

Worth 3 ♦ if not vulnerable but
you should pass if vulnerable,
just as you would as dealer.

The purpose of a weak
jump overcall is the
same as that of a pre-
emptive opening bid. It
makes life very difficult for the
opposition because it takes away
their bidding space. Even more so
after one of them has opened the
bidding, if you have a weak hand with a
long suit the chances are that the hand
will belong to your opponents more often
than not and they would much prefer to have an
uninterrupted run. to their chosen contract.

Meanwhile, again just as when opening with a pre-
empt, your good long suit affords you a good
degree of protection and your bid also acts as a
warning to partner that he cannot expect much
help from you except if your suit becomes trumps.

Weak jump overcalls are strongly recommended as
bridge is not a two-handed game where all that

matters is bidding to your best contract. It is a four-handed game in which making life difficult for your opponents is every bit as important.

And the good news is that, because you already play weak two-and three-level opening bids, you don't need to learn any new system to play them. just agree with your partner to respond exactly as if to the same opening bid and you won't go far wrong.

While we are on the subject of weak jump overcalls, let's also get bigger jumps out of the way. A double jump overcall such as 1 ♦ – 3 ♥ / ♠ is again just a pre-empt, showing a hand similar to one which would have opened 3 ♥ / ♠ had it been dealer. Likewise higher openings, though an overcall of four of a major can be a bit of a two-way call. Particularly if partner is a passed hand so that you feel that slam prospects are negligible, you might bid 4 ♠ over 1 ♣ / ♦ on either:

(a)
    ♠ KQJ109865
    ♥ J103
    ♦ 6
    ♣ 8

where you expect to go down but want to pre-empt as high as you can, or:

(b)
    ♠ AKQJ9765
    ♥ KJ10
    ♦ 5
    ♣ 10

where you need hardly anything from partner to make game but don't feel it is worth exploring slam possibilities.

other overcalls

There are three more types of overcall to consider. The first is a 2NT bid.

2NT could be used simply to show a hand which would have opened 2NT, with the added proviso that it must include a sure stopper in the suit opened. That is the easy option for anyone who doesn't want to take on any more artificial system for the moment. It does, however, come up extremely rarely, as you might imagine.

The popular alternative is to play a 2NT overcall as showing a genuine minor two-suiter or, more precisely, to show the two lowest unbid suits. This is known as the Unusual No Trump. So over 1♥/♠ a 2NT overcall shows clubs and diamonds, over 1♦ it shows clubs and hearts, and over 1♣ it shows diamonds and hearts.

By genuine two-suiter I mean at least five cards in each suit. The strength required is simply sufficient to compete at the three-level since that, of course, is the level to which you have committed your side. Typical 2NT overcalls of a 1♥/♠ opening might be:

(a)   ♠   5   (b)   ♠   4
           ♥   K3   ♥   A8
           ♦   QJ1074   ♦   KQ1087
           ♣   AJ975   ♣   AKJ62

With example (a) your intention is to pass partner's response. Holding example (b), you are too strong for that. Having heard partner's preference between your two suits, you might raise to the four-level to invite game.

(c)   ♠   A
                     ♥   A6
                     ♦   Q8764
                     ♣   J9742

Though having the same overall high card strength as example (a) and the same distribution, the quality of the suits would make it very dangerous to bid to the three-level with this hand. There is no guarantee that partner will have support for either of your suits and if the deal is a misfit you could be in big trouble. Better, then, to pass for now.

When responding to an Unusual 2NT overcall,

your first priority is to tell partner which of his two suits you prefer, usually by bidding it as cheaply as possible. Only with good support for one of the suits might you jump to show the suitability of your hand. Very rarely, you might bid a suit of your own or 3NT, but both of these require a very good reason to over-rule partner who has shown a hand really only suitable for play in one of his suits.

West	North	East	South
1 ♥	2NT	Pass	?

(a)
- ♠ Q8753
- ♥ J52
- ♦ K84
- ♣ 103

Bid 3 ♦, your preference between the minors. With your poor hand there is no reason to consider doing more.

(b)
- ♠ A8654
- ♥ 9854
- ♦ KJ63
- ♣ 5

Jump to 4 ♦ to invite game. You do not have much in the way of high cards but what you have, an ace plus trump honors, is very good. With four card support for one suit and a ruffing value in the other, game could be on if partner has a sound 2NT call.

(c)
♠ KQ108
♥ AQ98
♦ J52
♣ Q6

The rare handtype which can afford to raise to 3NT. Bear in mind that even as strong a hand as this does not guarantee that 3NT will make with the opening lead coming through your heart holding.

West	North	East	South
1♠	2NT	Dble	?

Here, the double merely shows a good hand and suggests that East/West might do well to double the final contract. With any of the examples above you would still make the same bid as before. Occasionally. however, you may have no preference between the minors. Holding:

♠ KJ754   or   ♠ A832
♥ Q642   ♥ 975
♦ J5   ♦ K63
♣ 108   ♣ J52

you might take advantage of the double to avoid having to choose between two roughly equal holdings. Simply pass and let partner decide. Often, this will make little difference but, if he happens to be 6-5 in his two suits rather than 5-5, he will be able to select the longer trump suit and thereby assure that the better contract is reached. Particularly where you would otherwise have had to choose between two doubletons, that could be very important.

The next overcall we need to consider is a 3NT bid. 1NT is natural, 2NT is Unusual, and 3NT is back to being natural again – good news. You could play bridge for years and never hold a balanced 25+ points when RHO opens the bidding. That doesn't mean that you will never want to overcall 3NT, merely that you will normally have a different handtype when you do so. A 3NT overcall is natural but tends to be based on a long suit which you hope will run and provide a lot of tricks. Over a 1♥ opening, these are typical 3NT bids:

(a) ♠ 76
     ♥ AQ
     ♦ AKQJ875
     ♣ Q3

(b) ♠ A7
     ♥ AJ2
     ♦ KQJ987
     ♣ A4

Actually, you might try it with a shade weaker hand than these two examples on occasion but the main point is that you have a long strong suit which is either running or has only one loser and you have a certain stopper in the enemy suit. While it is nice to have every suit covered, you can usually afford to be weak in at least sidesuit as LHO will lead his partner's suit unless he has a good reason to do otherwise. The weaker your long suit, however, the more careful you need to be that there is no glaring weakness elsewhere.

There is little to be said about responding to one of these bids. Usually your duty is just to put dummy down and hope that 3NT makes.

The final type of overcall we need to look at is a bid of the opponents' suit, i.e a cuebid. Traditionally, an overcall such as 1 ♥ – 2 ♥ showed any hand that wanted to drive to game, whether balanced, one-, two- or three-suited. That was pretty cumbersome and, frankly, had precious little merit.

In the tournament world many pairs use the immediate cuebid to show specific two-suited hands of moderate strength. you may well come across such methods as you play against new people. For the moment, however, I suggest a compromise. Keep he game-forcing nature of the traditional approach but play that the cuebid always shows a genuinely two-suited hand, i.e. at least 5-5. That way you get out of the way an awkward handtype which doesn't really fit conveniently anywhere else. So, over a 1 ♥ opening:

(a)   ♠ AQJ98   (b)   ♠ KQJ105
         ♥ 76   ♥ 4
         ♦ AKQ53   ♦ A
         ♣ A   ♣ AQJ1094

Either of these hands might bid 1 ♥ – 2 ♥, as they need so little for game that neither will be really comfortable stopping lower.

This will be a pretty rare call and, while it is possible to add artificial methods to discover which suits are held, it is not really necessary. Simplest is for responder to merely bid the cheapest suit which he can tolerate – in other words holds at least three cards in. If that is one of the overcaller's suits he can raise it, if not he bids one of the other suits and, since there were only ever three suits to choose from, it will be immediately apparent which two suits are held. All the responder needs to remember is that the sequence is game-forcing and he must keep faith with partner in that regard.

the takeout double

You will have noticed that there are several handtypes which cannot be shown by any type of overcall. Balanced hands with no stopper in the opponents' suit are a problem, as are single-suiters too strong for a simple overcall and also any good hand with no suit long or strong enough to overcall. All these are covered by one call – the takeout double!

Where a double is the first positive call made by your side it is for takeout, in other words, asking partner to bid something. His duty is first to tell you which suit, other than the one opened, he likes best and, second, what sort of all-round strength he has. accordingly, a double is the ideal solution when an opponent opens the bidding with a suit bid and the next player is strong enough to want to compete but has no clearcut descriptive bid available.

The minimum requirement for a takeout double of a one of a suit is the strength to have opened the bidding yourself. But you are asking partner to choose a suit in which to play and, the better your support for whichever suit that proves to be, the less high cards you need. The ideal shape for a takeout double is a 4-4-4-1 hand with shortage in the suit opened. That way, whichever suit partner bids you will have four card support. The further your actual hand deviates from that ideal distribution, the more high card strength you need to compensate.

All these would be about minimum for a double of a 1 ♥ opening.

(a) ♠ K1076
    ♥ 5
    ♦ AJ43
    ♣ KJ86

(b) ♠ A1085
    ♥ 94
    ♦ KQ7
    ♣ AJ42

(c) ♠ AQ6
    ♥ 973
    ♦ A854
    ♣ KQ5

If your general bidding style is aggressive you might choose to shade these requirements by a point or so but what is important is that the worse your distribution becomes the stronger you must be in high cards.

Note also that there is a difference between doubling a 1♣ opening, where partner can respond at the one-level whatever suit he chooses, and doubling 1♠, where you are asking him to go to the two-level. In the latter case you are pushing the bidding to a higher level so need to be correspondingly sounder in your doubling style.

The above hands are all examples of hands where you feel that you would like to bid but have nothing which you can overcall. This is the basic takeout

double type but you can also double on stronger
hands such as:

(d) ♠ AQ87   (e) ♠ AQ5
     ♥ 6   ♥ KQ8
     ♦ AK62   ♦ J976
     ♣ KQ85   ♣ AK9

(f) ♠ AKJ87   (g) ♠ AKJ975
     ♥ A3   ♥ A
     ♦ KQ64   ♦ AK65
     ♣ J6   ♣ Q4

Whereas hands (a), (b) and (c) will all accept
partner's choice but bid no further unless he has
shown a good hand by his response, the four later
examples all intend to bid on.

(a) Has the classic takeout double shape but
     has substantial extra high card strength.
     Whatever suit partner bids, you
     intend to raise to show your extra
     values.

(b) Would have overcalled
     1NT but is a shade too
     strong. The way to show
     that is to double then bid
     no trump as cheaply as
     possible over partner's
     response. This promises about 19-
     21 HCP, the next range up over a
     simple 1NT overcall.

To double and then jump in no trump would be stronger again, promising 22+ HCP.

(c) Has a good five card spade suit but is too strong for a simple overcall. Not to worry. Start by doubling then bid spades as cheaply as possible over partner's response. To double then over-rule partner's choice by bidding a new suit does not mean that you only had the other two suits and not the one he bid. No. It shows a five card suit of your own and the only sensible explanation for your making a takeout double instead of overcalling is that you were too strong to make a simple overcall.

This combination of double then bid a new suit shows 16+ HCP up to about 20. It is not forcing on partner to bid again but is highly encouraging.

(d) Is too strong even to double then bid the spades. Instead, start with a double then jump in spades on the next round. This shows at least five strong spades and 20+ HCP or the equivalent in distribution. It shows a very powerful hand which needs very little help if any to make game and is forcing for one round.

So, one of the decisions you always have to make is whether to double or to overcall.

If you have less than opening strength it is easy; you can overcall in a reasonable five card suit but are not strong enough to double.

If you have 16+ HCP or 19+ balanced with a stopper in the suit opened you are too strong to overcall so must start with a double.

In the range in between, about 12-15 HCP, the essential difference is that you overcall when you have a distinct preference for one suit over the others – when you want to tell partner something. You double when you do not have a clear preference so need to ask partner to pick the suit.

responding to a takeout double

The first thing to understand is that, if the third player passes, you must respond to partner's takeout double, however weak your hand. Imagine what will happen if you pass out of weakness. The fact that you are weak suggests that the opposition will have the majority of the high card strength. Meanwhile, the fact that partner made a takeout double, implying shortage in the enemy suit, suggests that they will have the greater trump length also. If that is the case, their contract is likely to make in some comfort, probably with overtricks. So, however dangerous it might appear to respond with a very weak hand, it will prove more expensive in the long run to pass. Usually, you will respond by bidding your longest suit. This is the standard scheme after the auction begins:

West	North	East	South
1 ♥	Dble	Pass	?

1 ♠/2 ♣/ ♦ = 0-7 HCP and is your longest suit.With two suits of equal length, tend to follow the same rules as for responding to an opening bid, i.e. bid the cheaper of four card suits, the higher of five card suits.

2 ♠/3 ♣/ ♦ = 8-11 HCP and is again your longest suit.

1NT = 6-10 HCP and shows a balanced hand with a good stopper in the opener's suit.

2NT = 11-12 HCP, a good stopper and a balanced hand.

Pass = Very rare but it shows very strong trumps and a positive desire to defend this contract.

With even stronger hands you can either jump all the way to game if you know where you want to play, on the assumption that partner has the basic takeout double type, or you can cuebid the opponents' suit.

Once again, we see that bidding the opponents' suit cannot mean that you want to play there. This is even more clear in this situation than in the previous ones we have noted. If, for example, you thought that you could make eight tricks with hearts as trumps, wouldn't you pass and defend 1♥ doubled rather than bid 2♥ and try to play there?

In this case, a cuebid of the opponents' suit means simply that you have the strength to go to game but are not sure which game will be best. You ask partner to bid his best suit and then each of you in turn can bid suits, or no trump, until you are satisfied that you have found the correct denomination in which to play. And, until game is reached, you can bid quietly, safe in the knowledge that partner is not allowed to pass.

Let's look at a few examples of responses in the following auction:

West	North	East	South
1 ♦	Dble	Pass	?

(a)
- ♠ J875
- ♥ 97
- ♦ 1084
- ♣ K1096

Bid 1 ♠, the cheaper of your two four card suits.

(b)
- ♠ KJ87
- ♥ 104
- ♦ A106
- ♣ J743

Respond 2 ♠, showing 8-11 points and, again, your favourite suit. Once you have the values to make a positive response, you can afford to be a little more flexible in your choice of response. Partner will tend to be more interested in the major suits than the minors, because it is easier to bid and make game in a major. Accordingly, even if a minor was cheaper, you would usually respond in the major.

Also, note that a four card major takes precedence over bidding 1NT to show a balanced hand. On the other hand, if your only four card suit was a minor, and you had a strong holding in opener's suit, you might prefer 1NT to a

bid of either two or three of the minor, again
because 3NT is easier than five of a minor.

(c)
        ♠ 986
        ♥ A107
        ♦ KJ96
        ♣ 1096

Bid 1NT, showing a balanced
6-10 HCP with a diamond
stopper. These diamonds are
not nearly good enough to pass
for penalties.

(d)
        ♠ 104
        ♥ A83
        ♦ KQJ108
        ♣ 987

This is the type of hand which is allowed to pass
the double. You are passing because you expect
to defeat 1 ♦ doubled by several tricks, not out of
weakness.

Because the pass always based on very good
trumps, the assumption is that they will be stronger
than opener's and that the only way he will make
many trump tricks is by ruffing. To prevent this, it is
usual for the doubler to lead a trump to start out
on the road to drawing all of declarer's small
trumps. Such a lead may prove unsuccessful if you
pass the double with unsuitable broken trump
holdings.

(e)

♠ AJ875
♥ K63
♦ A2
♣ 954

With an opening hand facing a partner who has promised at least opening strength, you want to get to game. With five cards in an unbid major, you can afford to jump straight to 4♠. Partner can be relied upon to have at least three spades unless he is very strong, in which case you can afford to get a little higher.

(f)

♠ Q76
♥ A1064
♦ A109
♣ KJ6

Again you have the values to bid to game, but which game is correct. It would be a mistake to jump to 3NT, for all your balanced hand and sure diamond stopper. Partner may have a singleton diamond and a diamond lead would leave you needing to run nine tricks without giving up the lead.

Equally, it would be wrong to jump to 4♥. Partner will have at least three hearts but need not have four.

Best is to cuebid 2♦. Now you

can each in turn bid your suits to try to find the best spot. For example:

West		East	
♠ Q76		♠ A875	
♥ A1064		♥ Q93	
♦ A109		♦ Q5	
♣ KJ6		♣ AQ42	

West	North	East	South
–	1♦	Dble	Pass
2♦	Pass	2♠	Pass
2NT	Pass	3♣	Pass
3♥	Pass	3NT	All Pass

Or, indeed, East might just raise 2NT to 3NT, safe in the knowledge that there can be no eight card major suit fit and that both hands are fairly balanced.

the doubler rebids

We have already seen how a player who doubles with a very big hand will bid again even when partner's response promises nothing.

Some general rules are:

When the response is a positive one, i.e. anything other than the lowest level of a new suit, a raise is invitational but any new suit or no trump bid is forcing.

When the response is a negative one, i.e. it is a new suit at the lowest available level, only a jump in a new suit or a cuebid of the opponents' suit by the doubler is forcing. All other bids are, however, constructive, and the responder should consider bidding on if his hand is reasonably suitable within the context of his initial weak response.

Remember, there is no need to worry that partner will get over-excited if you show some life on the second round of the auction. He has already heard your initial weak response so knows you cannot have more than about 7 HCP whatever you may bid later.

West	North	East	South
1 ♦	Dble	Pass	1 ♠
?			

(a)

- ♠ AQ75
- ♥ J854
- ♦ 10
- ♣ AQ32

Pass. You already showed opening values so have little to spare and game is hardly likely opposite a simple 1 ♠ response.

(b)
- ♠ AQ86
- ♥ K1054
- ♦ 3
- ♣ AK75

Raise to 2♠. This hand has an ace to spare for the initial double so can afford to bid again. A simple raise is sufficient as you only expect game to be good if partner has a maximum 1♠ response.

(c)
- ♠ AQ42
- ♥ AK98
- ♦ 6
- ♣ KQJ4

Raise to 3♠, a strong invitation. This time, with two spare tricks in your own hand, you want partner to bid game with anything useful.

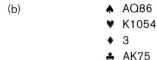

(d)
- ♠ AKJ2
- ♥ AQJ6
- ♦ 9
- ♣ KQJ5

Jump to 4♠. Now you need so little from partner that it may be difficult for him to bid game even if he has it if you only make an invitational bid.

(e)
- ♠ K62
- ♥ AQJ83
- ♦ A2
- ♣ KJ2

Bid 2♥. This shows a five card heart suit and a hand too strong for an initial overcall. It is not forcing but partner is expected to bid on if looking at useful values.

(f)
- ♠ K73
- ♥ AQJ8
- ♦ KJ6
- ♣ AKJ

Rebid 2NT, showing a balanced hand with a good diamond stopper and around 22-24 HCP. With a point or two less you would have doubled then rebid 1NT.

West	North	East	South
1♥	Dble	Pass	2♠
Pass	?		

(g)
- ♠ J854
- ♥ Q3
- ♦ AQ64
- ♣ A85

Pass. You only barely scraped up your initial double and partner's bid is only invitational, not forcing.

(h)
- ♠ K1083
- ♥ Q3
- ♦ AJ95
- ♣ AJ42

Raise to 3♠, invitational. Opposite a minimum 8/9 HCP, game is unlikely to be on, particularly as your ♥Q is of dubious value. If partner has a maximum 10/11 HCP there will be 25/26 HCP between the two hands and you will usually want to be in game so should make the invitational raise.

(i)

♠	K1074
♥	3
♦	AQ86
♣	AQ32

Raise straight to 4♠. You have 15 HCP plus a useful singleton. Had partner opened 1♠, you could have added three points for the singleton and can do likewise here as you have a known trump fit. Almost any 2♠ response should give a good play for game.

third hand bids

We have seen that if partner doubles and the next hand passes we must respond. What if the third hand does not pass?

The good news is that you are no longer obliged to bid as the double has already been removed. However, you should still bid if you have something to say. All jump bids and bids in no trump are pretty much the same as before. What about some of the weaker hands?

West	North	East	South
1♦	Dble	1♥	?

(a)
- ♠ J853
- ♥ 1064
- ♦ 973
- ♣ Q82

Pass. You have a weak hand which would only have responded because forced to do so. Take the opportunity afforded by East's bid to show that you are weak.

(b)
- ♠ KJ75
- ♥ 1064
- ♦ 973
- ♣ Q82

Bid 1♠. You are not ashamed of your hand and, if nothing else, would quite like a spade lead. You can afford to bid 1♠ because you are limited by your failure to jump to 2♠, so partner should not get over-excited.

West	North	East	South
1♥	Dble	2♥	?

(c)
- ♠ K83
- ♥ 74
- ♦ Q864
- ♣ A542

You would like to bid as you have have 9 HCP and must surely have a fit somewhere, but to bid a scrappy four card minor at the three-level is a little dangerous, partner not having guaranteed four card support for every suit. The solution is something we have not mentioned before. It is called a Responsive Double.

The idea is that when the opposition bid and support a suit at a low level you will rarely if ever want to double them for penalties. But at the same time, if they have a fit then so do you, if you can find it. A good agreement to have is that in an auction like the one above South should be able to respond with another takeout double, a Responsive Double, to say that he has some useful values but no long suit so is unsure where to play. The Responsive Double asks the first doubler to pick a suit.

Having agreed on the basic principle of the Responsive Double, you need to decide to what level it applies. In other words, having agreed that 1♥ – Dble – 2♥ – Dble is for takeout, what about 1♥ – Dble – 3♥ – Dble? I would play the double of any direct raise below game as takeout (or Responsive) but different people have their own ideas and the important thing is for you and partner to be on the same wavelength.

West	North	East	South
1♥	Dble	2♥	Pass
Pass	Dble		

What is going on here? North made a takeout double of 1♥ so can hardly suddenly have got a penalty double of 2♥. That would be a strange hand indeed. No. The second double is for takeout, just like the first. The only difference is that the second double promises a stronger hand. As responder is being asked to bid a level higher, the second double needs about an extra ace, e.g.

♠ AQ84
♥ 7
♦ AK93
♣ K863

If, instead, North bid 2♠ or 3♣/♦ at his second turn, he would be showing a five card or longer suit in a hand too strong for an initial overcall.

We have seen how you can make a takeout double then double a second time to show a better hand. Also, we have seen the double followed by a bid of a new suit or no trump to

show a hand too good for an immediate overcall.
There is just one more possibility to consider
before moving on to the next topic. What is the
meaning of a double in this kind of auction?

West	North	East	South
1 ♥	1 ♠	2 ♥	Pass
Pass	Dble		

The 1 ♠ overcall promises at least
five cards and a hand in the 8-15
HCP range. Now, what type of
hand would want to double 2 ♥,
when the opposition are
known to have a heart
fit?

It hardly makes
sense for this to be
a penalty double.
But 8-15 is quite a
wide range for the simple
overcall. To overcall then double on
the second round merely
shows a good hand for the
initial overcall and is for takeout.

Typical examples on the above auction would be:

(a)
                  ♠   AQJ85
                  ♥   9
                  ♦   K1064
                  ♣   A108

Double is much more flexible than 3♦ or repeating the spades when you have already promised five of them.

(b)

♠ Q106432
♥ 5
♦ AK6
♣ KQ8

With stronger spades you might just rebid them, but here you would not object to partner's bidding a five card minor so, again, the double is more flexible.

the opponents open 1NT

When an opponent opens 1NT, he tells his partner an awful lot about his hand in one go, leaving partner in a very good position to make future decisions for the partnership. This makes it relatively dangerous to overcall, as the player on your left knows his partner's strength and approximate shape and is well placed to make a penalty double if he has a few points and a promising holding in your suit.

Because of this, an overcall should either be based on a six card or longer suit or, if you do only have five cards, you should have some compensation in the form of distributional playing strength outside your main suit. In other words, to overcall with a 5-3-3-2 distribution is dangerous because you have no playing strength outside your high cards and main suit. If, on the other hand, your distribution is 5-4-3-1 or, even better, 5-5-2-1, then you have a second suit which offers the potential to be a source of playing tricks.

Even with suitable distribution, you should still have something approaching opening bid strength before you consider bidding over a strong no trump opening. These would be typical minimum overcalls:

(a)	♠ AQ9764	(b)	♠ AJ105
	♥ KQ4		♥ KQ1096
	♦ 87		♦ Q87
	♣ 109		♣ 5

Hand (a) has no useful outside distribution but has a fair six card suit so is worth a 2♠ overcall. Hand (d) has only a five card suit but the spades should come in handy so the hand can afford to overcall 2♥.

When partner bids over an opposing 1NT opening, any bid you make is constructive, unless he gets doubled when you are allowed to try to rescue him into your own suit. But bear in mind that the overcall did promise a good long suit so even now you should not often try a rescue act as often all you will achieve is to dig your side deeper into the mire.

West	North	East	South
1NT	2♥	Pass	?

(a)	♠ Q1097653
	♥ 8
	♦ J42
	♣ 104

2♠ will almost certainly be a better contract than 2♥ but still you must pass. If you bid 2♠ partner is entitled to expect a good hand with which game may be possible if he has support for your suit.

If, however, East doubles 2♥ for penalties, now you may run to 2♠. It would be very unlucky to find that 2♠ doubled was a worse spot than 2♥ doubled when you have such a long suit.

(b)
♠ AKJ86
♥ 85
♦ A97
♣ 632

Now 2♠ would be a perfectly reasonable choice, not quite forcing but highly encouraging.

It is highly unlikely that 2♥ would ever be doubled when you hold such a good hand but if it did happen I would not run because I would expect 2♥ doubled to make opposite my top cards.

If RHO opens 1NT and you do not have a long suit then your options are to pass or double. Unlike a double of a suit opening, a double of 1NT is for penalties, showing that you think your hand is better than the opener's. As you would imagine, with a strong no trump opening on your right, this does not come up all that often.

(a)
- ♠ KQ10
- ♥ AJ97
- ♦ K108
- ♣ Q109

If RHO opens 1NT, you must just pass. There is nothing you can overcall and your hand is no better than opener's so you cannot afford to double.

(b)
- ♠ AKQ
- ♥ QJ106
- ♦ A85
- ♣ K97

Now you can double. 19 HCP means that you are stronger than the opener and with two nice sequences you have a choice of safe and attractive leads.

(c)
- ♠ KQJ1096
- ♥ A86
- ♦ A3
- ♣ 98

You could also double with a hand of this type, even though in terms of high cards you are weaker than the opener. The point is that you can lead a spade honor and immediately establish enough tricks to defeat 1NT doubled. And if partner has a couple of high cards including a club stopper you will score much better defending 1NT doubled than by bidding and playing 2♠.

When partner doubles 1NT you will usually pass, knowing that he has a very strong hand. The only time that you might bid is with a weak distributional hand. To run to 2 ♥ with:

♠ 8
♥ 1087653
♦ 9754
♣ 62

is perfectly sensible and will be the correct thing to do whenever partner just has a big balanced hand. If he has a long strong suit and could have beaten 1NT doubled on his own he will be unhappy and it is partly because he will quite often hold that latter type of hand that you should not overdo the running from 1NT doubled.

conventional defenses to 1NT

It is all very well to overcall when you hold a six card suit but, as we have seen, if your suit is only five cards in length it is preferable to hold a second suit in reserve to add extra playing strength. If you are going to have two suits, why not find a way of showing two suits, thereby giving partner a choice and so increasing the chance of finding a sensible trump suit?

In the tournament world, it seems that there are almost as many different artificial defenses to 1NT in use as there are playing. It is way beyond the scope of this book to look in detail at these but you should at least be aware of their existence.

The thing all these defenses have in common is that a natural bid is given up to do different and, hopefully, more useful work. The simplest is the Landy convention. Playing Landy, a 2♣ overcall of 1NT is used to show both major suits − usually at least 5-4. If you want to bid clubs you have to bid 3♣ instead.

In response to the 2♣ overcall, partner usually bids his better major. With equal length he can bid 2♦ as a relay to ask the overcaller to bid his longer, or better, suit. These would be typical Landy 2♣ overcalls:

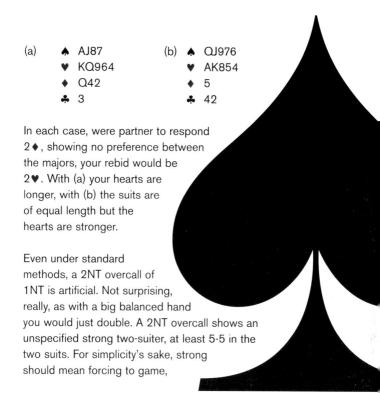

(a) ♠ AJ87   (b) ♠ QJ976
     ♥ KQ964   ♥ AK854
     ♦ Q42   ♦ 5
     ♣ 3   ♣ 42

In each case, were partner to respond
2♦, showing no preference between
the majors, your rebid would be
2♥. With (a) your hearts are
longer, with (b) the suits are
of equal length but the
hearts are stronger.

Even under standard
methods, a 2NT overcall of
1NT is artificial. Not surprising,
really, as with a big balanced hand
you would just double. A 2NT overcall shows an
unspecified strong two-suiter, at least 5-5 in the
two suits. For simplicity's sake, strong
should mean forcing to game,

e.g.

        ♠ KQJ108
        ♥ A3
        ♦ AQJ109
        ♣ 8

You can go quite some time without having an
opportunity to use this bid, just as with the
immediate cuebid over a one of a suit opening
which shows essentially the same type of hand.
A final thought: given the rarity of the penalty

double of a strong no trump, many tournament players prefer to use a double in an artificial sense. If you want to keep all your two-level overcalls natural then double could show some kind of two-suiter, perhaps both majors or both minors. Alternatively, if one of the defenses which uses some of the two-level bids in an artificial sense takes your fancy, you could use double to show an unspecified single-suited hand.

Up to now, we have always assumed that we were bidding in second seat, immediately over the opening bid. But sometimes the second and third hands will both pass and we will be last to speak. Should we keep the bidding alive and if so how, or should we pass it out.

bidding in fourth seat

The fourth seat is known as the balancing position and, while most of our basic rules still apply, they need some modification as there are different considerations from when bidding in second seat. Firstly, we need to look at the meaning of some of our overcalls.

The jump overcall should no longer be weak. The main purpose of a weak jump overcall is to pre-empt the opposition. Once they have passed the deal out at the one-level this becomes much less important. Better to play jump overcalls in the pass-out seat as intermediate. In other words:

West	North	East	South
West	*North*	*East*	*South*
1 ♦	Pass	Pass	2 ♠

Should show a decent six card suit and sound opening values, around the 12-15 range; e.g.

♠ AQ10975
♥ K8
♦ A65
♣ 72

Many moderate balanced hands would not fit into any convenient bid if we did not modify the strength of a 1NT overcall. Various ranges are played around the world but something like 12-15 makes good sense. Also, while it is still preferable to have a stopper in the opponents' suit, you might occasionally decide that 1NT was the best option even without one, hoping that partner, who is sitting over the opener, may have what you need.

West	North	East	South
1♦	Pass	Pass	1NT

Typical examples would be:

(a)
- ♠ A75
- ♥ K3
- ♦ QJ85
- ♣ K974

(b)
- ♠ A8
- ♥ QJ4
- ♦ 10975
- ♣ AK85

In the latter case there is only a partial diamond stopper but double is hardly sensible with only five cards in the majors.

If you hold a stronger balanced hand you star with a double. A hand in the 16-18 range, which would have overcalled 1NT in second seat, doubles then rebids no trump at the minimum level over partner's response.

What about 19-21? This range causes a bit of a problem, particularly if partner's response to the double was at the two-level. With 2NT showing 16-18, you can hardly jump to 3NT to show 19-21 or you will reach far too many hopeless games. It is time for another bid to change its meaning, namely the 2NT overcall.

In fourth seat you need a natural 2NT overcall just to enable you to fit in all the different strong balanced ranges. Accordingly, instead of showing a two-suiter, 2NT here shows 19-21 balanced. Now double then a jump in no trump is 22+ and everything is a lot more comfortable.

A good idea is to play that you respond to any natural 1NT or 2NT overcall exactly as you would to a natural 1NT or 2NT opening bid, making allowance only for the different strengths promised by the different bids. So if you play 2NT – 3♣ as Stayman, play it the same way when 2NT is an overcall, and so on.

the takeout double

A balancing double promises the same shape as
would the same call in second seat but the
standard approach is to allow a double to be
made on hands about a king lighter than in second
seat.

West	North	East	South
1♦	Pass	Pass	?

(a)
- ♠ AJ64
- ♥ K853
- ♦ 92
- ♣ Q107

In second seat, this would have been a routine
pass. Here, it is worth a double. The point is that, if
you pass that is it, the auction is over. Partner may
well have a fair hand but the wrong shape to allow
an immediate bid in second seat. By doubling you
'protect' his pass and give him a second chance.
(Protection is another name sometimes given to
bidding in the fourth seat.)

(b)
- ♠ Q1096
- ♥ KJ83
- ♦ 7
- ♣ Q964

Again you would be well short of a double in
second seat but, with your ideal distribution, can
double in fourth seat.

It is clear that, if a takeout double can be made on as few as 8/9 HCP, the responder to the double has to pull in his horns and not bid on the assumption that the double promises opening strength. The rule is that, because the double can be made about a king lighter than usual, strength showing responses require about a queen or king more than normal to compensate.

Obviously, the minimum strength required for a simple response cannot change as you must still respond even with nothing. However, the upper limit should be raised so that, where the auction:

West	North	East	South
1♦	Dble	Pass	2♠

might promise about 8-11 HCP, the sequence:

West	North	East	South
1♦	Pass	Pass	Dble
Pass	2♠		

should show 10-13 or even a shade better than that.

Likewise, a 1NT response to a second seat double promises 6-10 HCP while the same response to a fourth seat double should be more like 8-12, and so on.

One other call which is affected by the altered situation is the penalty pass. Where, facing a second seat double, you needed almost solid trumps before you could afford to convert the double and play for penalties by passing, now you are sitting over the prospective declarer and may pass more freely on broken holdings, knowing that all his trump finesses are doomed to failure. So:

West	North	East	South
1 ♥	Pass	Pass	Dble
Pass	?		

(a)
- ♠ Q104
- ♥ A8754
- ♦ K83
- ♣ KJ2

Bid 2NT. Your trumps are not good enough for a penalty pass. But:

(b)
- ♠ A7
- ♥ KJ975
- ♦ K63
- ♣ Q54

Pass. You can hope for quite a lucrative penalty when all your trumps are sitting poised to capture declarer's high trumps. Note how different the situation is because you are sitting over declarer. If you were on his right, he might have ♥AQ1086 sitting over you and you would make far fewer tricks.

the simple overcall

In some ways, this is a slightly more complex problem than when you are trying to decide whether to double or overcall 1NT. The very fact that you are thinking about an overcall suggests that you have a long suit and, therefore, must have a relatively short suit elsewhere.

While this may not be of too much concern when you hold a good hand, if you are below opening bid strength you might like to consider not only what your side can make but what your opponents might bid and make if given a second chance.

There are two factors to bear in mind. Firstly, your length in the opener's suit. The shorter partner was in this suit, the more likely he would be to have overcalled or doubled in second seat. Accordingly, the greater your length in the suit, the less likely it is that partner has a good hand. Obviously, the weaker he is the greater the risk that the deal belongs to your opponents.

Secondly, what about your length in the majors and in particular spades? If partner had a few high cards and a five card spade suit, he might have overcalled. His failure to do so should set alarm bells ringing if you are short in spades. Perhaps you will reopen the bidding and be outbid by opponents who own the top-ranking suit. You could even find them bidding and making a game when you could have left them to play at the one-level.

West	North	East	South
1♦	Pass	Pass	?

(a)

♠ 108754
♥ A93
♦ K7
♣ K86

Bid 1♠. At the one-level, any five card suit is now good enough to bid.

(b)
♠ KQ87
♥ A4
♦ 108
♣ J9764

At the two-level, you would still like to have a better suit than those clubs. Double is also out because of the shortage in hearts. Bid 1♠. In the pass-out seat, you are allowed to bid a reasonable four card major if nothing else is appealing.

(c)
♠ AK86
♥ 75
♦ 94
♣ AQ1053

This time you can overcall 2♣ and, if you get a second chance, bid your spades next time.

(d)

♠ 86
♥ AJ875
♦ 95
♣ QJ65

My vote is for pass! The problem is the spade shortage, strongly suggesting that the opposition either have a significant advantage in high card strength or have a spade fit. Either way you will be outbid if you overcall. Better to defend 1♦.

This is the nightmare scenario if you overcall 1♥:

```
                  ♠ J9
                  ♥ KQ43
                  ♦ QJ1042
                  ♣ K7
    ♠ AK74                      ♠ Q10532
    ♥ 6                         ♥ 1092
    ♦ AK863                     ♦ 7
    ♣ A105                      ♣ 9843
                  ♠ 86
                  ♥ AJ875
                  ♦ 95
                  ♣ QJ65
```

West	North	East	South
1♦	Pass	Pass	1♥
Dble	2/3♥	2/3♠	Pass
4♠	All Pass		

You could have left West to struggle in 1 ♦, instead of which you allow him to make a takeout double of your overcall and East appreciates the value of his hand so bids the spades. Suddenly you find yourself defending an untouchable game contract.

This is a worst case scenario, of course, but it will be quite common for East/West to outbid you in a partscore battle so always look at your length in spades and, to a lesser extent, hearts, before balancing with an overcall on a weakish hand.

weak two bids

Traditionally, two-level opening bids were played as showing very powerful hands, but these came up relatively rarely and more and more people have turned to playing weak two bids. While a weak two bid helps your own constructive bidding by allowing you to open and describe an extra handtype which is not catered for by traditional methods, the biggest virtue of weak two bids is their pre-emptive effect and the problems which they cause for the opposition.

It is imperative, therefore, to agree a sensible defense to these weak two openers. There are a number of artificial methods doing the rounds, but the majority of experienced players treat them essentially 'as ones', i.e. use the same basic methods as over a one of a suit opening bid.

There is a problem with this approach and it is that there is far less space available in which to explore all the possible options and, in particular, to make invitational bids.

overcalls

There is little that you can do where overcalling is concerned. You are, of course, overcalling a level higher than after a one-level opening so need a correspondingly higher minimum before you can bid.

If 2 ♥ is opened on your right you can bid 2♠ on:

- ♠ AQJ86
- ♥ A3
- ♦ J102
- ♣ 974

and 3 ♦ on:

- ♠ AK
- ♥ 1052
- ♦ AQJ1054
- ♣ J8

but must pass holding:

- ♠ KQ1094
- ♥ A3
- ♦ 1065
- ♣ 976

which would have been a routine 1♠ overcall of a 1 ♥ opening.

It is not normal to pre-empt over a pre-empt. In other words, if RHO starts with a pre-empt, any jump bid you make should be strong. There is no reason to pre-empt yourself when an opponent has already announced weakness. So a jump overcall such as 2♥ – 3♠ should be strong, perhaps:

- ♠ AKJ875
- ♥ 743
- ♦ AQ10
- ♣ K7

such a jump is not forcing but is highly invitational.

For obvious reasons, you may not wish to go beyond 3NT if your main suit is a minor as that could be the best game. Accordingly, a 3♣/♦ overcall covers a pretty wide range of hands and you need to bear this in mind when deciding on your response to an overcall. 2♥ – 3♦ might be as little as:

- ♠ K8
- ♥ 76
- ♦ AKJ965
- ♣ 987

or as much as:

- ♠ AK
- ♥ 75
- ♦ AKJ965
- ♣ Q3

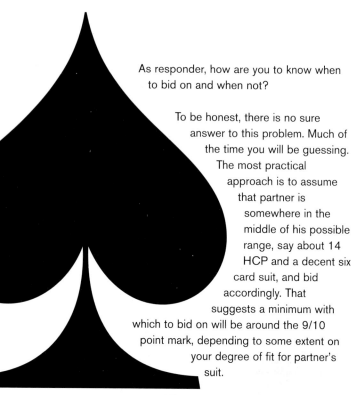

As responder, how are you to know when to bid on and when not?

To be honest, there is no sure answer to this problem. Much of the time you will be guessing. The most practical approach is to assume that partner is somewhere in the middle of his possible range, say about 14 HCP and a decent six card suit, and bid accordingly. That suggests a minimum with which to bid on will be around the 9/10 point mark, depending to some extent on your degree of fit for partner's suit.

Alas, this means that you will sometimes miss a fair game and on other occasions bid a thoroughly bad one, but with no room in which to explore, what can you do? That is why people pre-empt.

When you do decide to bid on, bids mean pretty much what you might expect. Raises below game are invitational, new suits are natural, at least five cards, and are forcing if below game, while a bid of the opener's suit asks for further information – as often as not with no trump in mind if partner can provide a stopper.

The other overcall to consider is one in no trump. Both 2NT and 3NT are natural bids, though they tend to be based on different handtypes.

A 3NT overcall will tend to be similar to a 3NT overcall of a one-level opening, strong and with stoppers in the opponents' suit but based on a long semi-solid minor.

A 2NT overcall is much more like a 1NT overcall of a one bid, balanced with a sure stopper in the enemy suit. The range is pretty much the same as well, around 16-18, though you might stretch a suitable 15 or downgrade a poor 19. It is best to respond to 2NT using exactly the same methods as if facing a 2NT opening, just making allowances for the different strengths promised by the two calls.

the takeout double

When partner makes a takeout double there is still less room in which to define your strength. If, for example, partner doubles a 2♠ opening, you have to respond 3♥ on both:

♠ 742
♥ 10864
♦ J84
♣ 432

and:

♠ A42
♥ KQJ6
♦ 864
♣ 743

How on earth is the doubler to know whether you are bidding only because you were forced to do so and hate the whole thing or actually have a pretty good hand as with the second example?

Playing standard methods there is no way to distinguish between the two handtypes. This is a serious problem and has resulted in a number of schemes being developed to try to resolve it. Some, for example, use 3♣ and 3♦ as weak and strong takeout bids so that the initial bidder tries to define his strength and responder can decide whether to bid game or settle for a partscore.

All these schemes which involve two different takeout bids suffer from the serious flaw of leaving too many simple hands unbiddable. If you use 3♣ as a takeout bid, for example, what do you do when you pick up 14 HCP and a six card club suit?

The most popular solution at tournament level is to employ something called Lebensohl responses to the takeout double. In this scheme double is the only takeout call but responder has a way of showing whether he is very weak or has reasonable values. The scheme utilises an artificial 2NT response to the double and goes something like this:

West	North	East	South
2♠	Dble	Pass	?

2NT =	A puppet, demanding that partner bid 3♣
3♣/♦/♥ =	Natural and invitational, around 7-11 HCP
3♠ =	Cuebid, game values with four hearts and a spade stopper
3NT =	To play, game values and a spade stopper but not four hearts

Higher responses show stronger and usually more shapely hands and are forcing to game.
So the problem of responder's range is greatly

reduced as any response other than 2NT promises a fair hand.

After any response other than 2NT, bidding proceeds naturally. The doubler can choose which game to play opposite the cuebid, and decide whether to bid on opposite one of the invitational responses in a new suit.

What happens where responder's bid is 2NT? Initially, the doubler should assume that he is facing 0-6 HCP. Unless he has a very strong hand which might still be interested in game even opposite such a weak hand, he normally does as requested and bids 3♣. If, instead, he makes any other bid, he shows a big hand and responder should strain to bid on at the slightest excuse.

West	North	East	South
2♠	Dble	Pass	2NT
Pass	3♣	Pass	?

Pass =   0-6 with clubs the longest suit

3♦/♥ =   0-6 and natural

3♠ =   Game values, four hearts but no spade stopper

3NT =   Balanced hand with game values, not four hearts and no spade stopper

So not only does Lebensohl allow you to differentiate between weak and reasonable hands, if you play the full scheme you can also distinguish between various kinds of balanced hands with game values, leaving the initial doubler to make the final decision. I have to confess that the different cuebids are a bit complicated and you could always forget about them to start with and just use the 2NT response as a way to show a weak hand.

The cost of this convention is relatively low, as long as you both remember it, relative to its benefits, as all you give up is a natural 2NT response to the takeout double. Best with such a hand is to either pass for penalties or gamble a jump to 3NT, as seems more appropriate.

If the weak opening is 2 ♥, the scheme still applies. The main difference is that you can bid 2♠ with a weak hand with spades so 2NT is usually a weak hand with clubs or diamonds. If you like, you can differentiate between an immediate response of 3♠ and 2NT followed by 3♠, but I leave those of you who like a lot of system to work out the details for yourselves.

Let's look at a couple of examples of how it all works. In each case, LHO opens 2♠ and partner doubles.

(a)   ♠   642
            ♥   K94
            ♦   87
            ♣   J8643

Respond 2NT, requesting 3♣ from partner. If he obliges, you intend to pass the 3♣ bid.

(b)

    ♠ J64
    ♥ 97
    ♦ KQ87
    ♣ A542

Respond 3♦, the stronger of your four card suits. The immediate suit response is not forcing but promises fair values, around 7-11 points.

RHO opens 2♠ and you double holding:

    ♠ Q5
    ♥ KJ97
    ♦ AQJ2
    ♣ A104

If partner responds 2NT you just bid 3♣ as requested then, if he follows up with 3♦/♥ you pass, trusting him to be weak.

If the initial response is 3♥ you raise to 4♥, knowing that partner has some useful high cards and that there is an eight card or better heart fit. If the response is 3♣/♦, bid 3♠, asking partner to bid 3NT if he has a spade stop. You know that there will usually be game values between the two hands because of the immediate response in a suit, and your balanced hand suggests that 3NT may be easier than five of a minor unless partner is very distributional.

bidding in fourth seat

There is little change if you are considering bidding in fourth seat after two passes. You can bid slightly more aggressively here than in second position, particularly when doubling, to protect partner's pass which might sometimes be based on a fair hand with the wrong distribution to come in second seat.

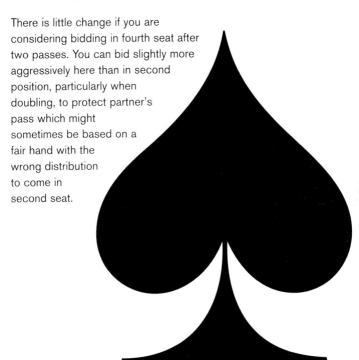

three-level openings

Three-level opening bids are pre-emptive in nature, based on a good long suit but not many high cards. Their mission is to make life difficult for the opposition and that is exactly what they do. Even the very best players cannot judge right all the time when an opponent pre-empts and there is no magic system which will work all the time. Why not? Because such a system is impossible. There simply isn't room to have the same degree of accuracy if you have to start bidding at the three-level over an enemy pre-empt as when you can have an uninterrupted run starting at the one-level. Pre-empts sometimes work, that is why people use them.

However, if you play a sound system and, even more important perhaps, take the right philosophical approach to the situation, you can hope to get sensible results most of the time and occasional very good ones. The philosophy I am talking about is really just an acceptance that the pre-empt will sometimes fix you, making it impossible to reach the ideal contract. Don't worry. Rather than continually strive for the best possible result, settle for the best result practically possible each time. Sure, you will miss some wonderful contracts this way but you will also avoid a lot of the disasters which are lurking just around the corner.

The second thing to consider is that you are not the only one under pressure, so is partner. Where you can do so, try to relieve that pressure; take decisions yourself where it is reasonable to do so and make clear, understandable, bids, rather than torture him with a too subtle approach.

Thirdly, bear in mind that the pre-emptive opening has promised a distributional hand. If in doubt about how high to bid consider that there may well be bad breaks around so err on the side of caution.

As far as methods are concerned, you will come across any number of people who will swear by this or that convention, and there are plenty of options doing the rounds. But the vast majority of the world's experts play what I would describe as a natural defense to pre-empts.

The recommended defense is to pretty much treat three-level openings as ones. In other words, double is for takeout, overcalls, including 3NT, are natural, and a cuebid of the opponents' suit shows a two-suited hand. Takeout doubles have the merit of simplicity and of flexibility. Any method which uses an alternative takeout bid loses a great deal of flexibility and that is a very serious loss when you are already under such pressure.

If there was a problem making invitational bids after the opposition opened with a weak two bid, the problem is even more serious when they open at the three-level. Basically, there is no room at all in which to invite game so if partner overcalls or doubles you have to make the decision yourself.

The traditional approach here is that when considering a bid over an opposing pre-empt you assume that partner will have six or seven points and bid (or not) accordingly. Now responder discounts the first six or seven points in his hand, on the assumption that you have already allowed for his having so much, and only makes a positive bid if he has something extra. This is obviously not perfect, but it is the best anyone has come up with to date.

overcalls

Just as when defending against a two-level opening, you need to remember that you are entering the bidding at a higher level than over a one-bid. The minimum requirement for a three-level overcall would be something like:

♠ AQJ87	or	♠ AJ10874
♥ AK4		♥ AQ3
♦ 653		♦ 54
♣ 82		♣ 72

or:

Either would be close to a minimum 3♠ overcall, around 11+ HCP with a six card suit or 14+ if only a five card suit.

You might want to overcall with:

   ♠ AJ9875
   ♥ A32
   ♦ 54
   ♣ 64

but bidding on such weak hands makes it very difficult for partner to judge when to bid on. The chances are that whenever you could have made 3♠ partner will raise to game and you will go down a lot of the time.

Holding:

   ♠ AKQJ98
   ♥ AK2
   ♦ K7
   ♣ 64

Overcall 4♠ rather than 3♠. You cannot underwrite game, of course, but this is an example of taking pressure off partner. You need so little from him to make game when holding an 8/9 trick hand that it will be difficult for him to know when to bid on.

responding to an overcall

As we have said, responder to the overcall should discount his first six or seven points on the basis that partner has already assumed them.

	West	North	East	South
	3♦	3♠	Pass	?

(a)
- ♠ Q63
- ♥ J85
- ♦ 1073
- ♣ A543

Pass. You have a couple of useful high cards and fair trump support but otherwise your hand is nothing special and, once you have discounted the first six or seven points there is nothing left.

(b)
- ♠ Q63
- ♥ A85
- ♦ 1073
- ♣ A1085

Raise to 4♠. This time you have more than partner has allowed for so, with reasonable trump support, can raise to game.

(c)
- ♠ 83
- ♥ AQ104
- ♦ K974
- ♣ QJ8

Bid 3NT. You have poor support for spades but plenty of high cards and a sure diamond stopper.

(d)
- ♠ K3
- ♥ A7
- ♦ 964
- ♣ AQJ875

Bid 4♣. A bid of a new suit is natural and, if below game, forcing. If partner repeats his spades you may play there but until he does so it is not clear that spades is the right trump suit. Bidding 4♣ offers him an alternative.

(e)
- ♠ KJ64
- ♥ KQ3
- ♦ A8
- ♣ Q1094

Bid 4♦. This cuebid shows spade support but says that you are too strong just to raise to game and want to invite slam.

Traditionally, this cuebid also guaranteed a diamond control, as in the above example. A modern expert treatment is to cuebid the opponents' suit on any hand which wants to invite slam in partner's suit, irrespective of whether it includes a control in the suit opened. If playing that way, you could also cuebid 4♦ even if your minor suits were reversed.

This is quite a good idea and fits in well with the general principles we saw earlier at lower levels with the unassuming cuebid opposite a one-level overcall. It is not, however, a mainstream agreement, and you would certainly not expect it to be played by a complete stranger unless you specifically discussed it in advance.

A 3NT overcall is natural and, with no room to distinguish between the two handtypes, could be based on a strong balanced hand or a long minor. Either way, it must include a stopper in the suit opened, for obvious reasons. The minimum requirement to overcall 3NT on a balanced hand would be around 16 HCP, much as at a lower level. But a stronger balanced hand would also have to make the same bid, even with 24 or 25 HCP. After all, what else can you do?

Specialised responses are available to try to differentiate between the different handtypes and strengths when responder wants to bid on, using a 4♣ response as an enquiry. This is really beyond the scope of this book, however, and I leave regular partnerships who like system to work out their own scheme.

the takeout double

The requirements for a takeout double are little changed from those at a lower level. Though you are bidding at a higher level, any opening hand of the appropriate shape has to double. The problem is that if you are short in the suit opened and pass because you only have 12/13 HCP, partner may have the same kind of strength but not be short enough in the enemy suit to double. You could find yourselves defending three of a suit when you are cold for game your way. The hand with shortage in the suit opened has to strain to come into the bidding, therefore.

These would be typical minimum doubles of a 3♦ opening:

♠	AQ64	and	♠	KJ8
♥	K853		♥	AQ104
♦	7		♦	93
♣	QJ84		♣	KJ95

Note that, as usual, greater high card strength is required as compensation the further the hand gets away from the ideal shape for a takeout double.

responding to a takeout double

The scheme is remarkably similar to that facing a double of a one-level opening. Firstly, responder must bid something however weak his hand. You do not want to defend a doubled contract when you are very weak and partner is likely to be short

in the trump suit. Far too often that will lead to
−730 or −470.

You can, however, pass for penalties on much lesser
trump holdings than when facing a one-level double.
This would be a sound pass of 3 ♦ doubled:

    ♠ A64
    ♥ 83
    ♦ K1087
    ♣ J954

With only 8 HCP there is no reason to imagine
that you can make a game but, with one or
probably two trump tricks plus an outside ace, you
should get a fair penalty from 3 ♦ doubled.

To respond 3NT, you would want a fair hand as
partner may have minimum opening bid strength
with shortage in the suit opened. This might be a
minimum 3NT bid opposite a double of 3 ♥:

    ♠ K87
    ♥ AJ8
    ♦ QJ43
    ♣ 1096

There is no guarantee of making 3NT but if partner
has anything to spare you should have fair chances.

Most of the time you will respond in a new suit.
Bid as cheaply as possible with a weak hand but
jump with 8/9 working points upwards – much as

you would opposite a one-level double. Let me explain what I mean by working points.

```
♠  AJ87
♥  965
♦  K1086
♣  105
```

Facing a double of either a 3♣ or 3♥ opening, this hand is worth a jump to 4♠. What high cards you have are all in partner's suits, so nothing is wasted.

Conversely:

```
♠  A987
♥  KJ3
♦  10864
♣  J53
```

If the opening bid was 3♥, almost half your strength is opposite partner's shortage so not pulling its weight. He will need to be very strong to avoid losers in the minors where you have length but no strength. Though you have 9 HCP, 4♠ is too much. I would pass, figuring that we have enough strength to defeat 3♥ doubled, but that with only five working points 4♠ is unlikely our way. Second choice would be a cautious 3♠.

Just as at a lower level, if responder has game values but does not wish to commit himself to a trump suit, he can cuebid the opponents' suit to ask the doubler to choose. When a double of 3♦ comes round to you and you hold:

- ♠ AJ75
- ♥ K1086
- ♦ J4
- ♣ Q95

Respond 4♦. Partner will normally bid his better major suit, even with five clubs and only a four card major. Only if his only suit is clubs will he respond 5♣, and in that case he will surely hold at least five and there will be no 4-4 major suit fit. Of course, you are allowed to jump in a four card suit in response to the double, but you only do so when you have only one major so see no prospect of an alternative game. Partner's double did not guarantee four cards in every suit so when you have two possible trump suits it makes sense to play safe by asking him to choose.

the direct cuebid

A direct cuebid of an opening pre-empt shows a genuinely two-suited hand, at least 5-5 in the two suits. Traditionally, this was played as a very strong bid, in much the same way as a cuebid of a one-level opening. A typical example for a 3♦ – 4♦ cuebid would be:

♠ AKQ87
♥ AQ10986
♦ –
♣ J5

Clearly, a takeout double would be inappropriate as you would hate to hear partner bid clubs or pass for penalties. Equally, to make an overcall of either 3♥ or 4♥ could lead to a grossly inferior contract if partner has spade support but heart shortage. The cuebid solves the problem nicely.

In response to the cuebid, you normally bid the cheapest suit for which you have tolerance, rather than your longest suit.
For example, after 3♣ – 4♣, holding:

♠ K875
♥ 64
♦ Q108
♣ J432

Respond 4♦, your preference if partner has both red suits. If he actually has the majors he will bid 4♥ and now you can convert to 4♠, safe in the knowledge that if he doesn't have diamonds he must have spades.

A more modern approach which is popular in the tournament world is to play the cuebid as merely showing a reasonable two-suiter but not necessarily so strong. The theory is that what really matters is to play with the correct trump suit and if that occasionally leads to playing a level higher than you would really like it is a price worth paying. Rather than guess which suit to overcall, this would be a cuebid of a 3♣/♦ opening.

♠ AQ1098
♥ AQJ64
♦ 7
♣ 83

You are not strong enough to insist on game yet 3♥ or 3♠ could go badly wrong. At least the cuebid means that you will have a sensible trump fit.

Under this scheme, a cuebid of a minor would show both majors until proven otherwise, and a cuebid of a major would show the other major plus an unspecified minor. Responder would still normally choose between the two suits shown. With both majors, the cuebid could be quite limited, as in the last example. But you might also cuebid with the 'wrong' two-suiter if very strong. So:

West	North	East	South
3♦	4♦	Pass	4♥
Pass	4♠		

Initially, 4♦ showed a moderate major two-suiter and South responded with that in mind, selecting his better major. The 4♠ bid means that North did not, in fact, hold both majors but actually held the black suits. When you cuebid with other than the expected two suits, you should go back to the traditional strong version of the cuebid as you will frequently end up at the five level.

In conjunction with the cuebid, whichever style you choose, a 4NT overcall of three of a major should be played as showing a good minor two-suiter, at least 5-5. So 4NT is 'unusual', just as over a 1 ♥/♠ opening.

bidding in fourth seat

As at lower levels, you can bid on slightly weaker hands in fourth suit if three of a suit is passed round to you. In particular, if you are short in the suit opened there is a good chance that partner is sitting there licking his lips at the prospect of a reopening double. Holding:

- ♠ AJ75
- ♥ J864
- ♦ K873
- ♣ 6

You would not have doubled a 3♣ opening in second seat but should do so in fourth position. Imagine that partner has something like:

- ♠ K85
- ♥ A53
- ♦ A64
- ♣ K1075

He will pass a takeout double and the contract is likely to go about three down with no game on for your side. Take away an ace and 3♣ doubled is still going down quite easily.

Of course, partner will not always have a good trump holding with which to pass the double. Sometimes he will just have a balanced or semi-balanced hand which was not strong enough to bid immediately. If he makes allowances for the fact that you are doubling in the balancing position and makes a cautious response any time he has a close decision, you should not get in too many difficulties so long as you have the right shape. You would not mind if he jumped to game with:

♠ Q94
♥ KQ105
♦ A102
♣ 853

if you doubled a 3♣ opening. Game is not certain but it has good chances with most of the missing strength marked on your right.

Conversely, if you have length in the opponents' suit, be careful about coming in. The more length you hold the less that leaves for partner. When he is short in their suit he is unlikely to have a good hand as he would then have bid himself in second position. So, after 3♦ is passed round to you:

♠ AJ7
♥ Q853
♦ K86
♣ A97

You have 14 HCP but no playing strength as your hand is too balanced. It is just possible that partner could hold a similar hand and that 3NT is on, but far more likely he is weakish and if you bid you risk going down.

Imagine that partner has:

♠ Q94
♥ K106
♦ Q9
♣ J8643

If you pass you have very good chances of defeating 3 ♦, given that you have the majority of the high cards and two probable trump tricks as dummy will usually hold a singleton trump, allowing declarer to finesse only once.

If, on the other hand, you bid, you are unlikely to find a safe resting place. And RHO is marked with a strong hand short in his partner's suit. If, for example, you make a takeout double and partner responds 4♣, he may well be doubled and go a couple down – a serious loss when you could have gone plus by passing out 3 ♦.

conclusion

We have covered a lot of ground in what is quite a short book and, alongside the basic defensive bidding methods, I have introduced some quite modern ideas. There is no need for you to take everything on board at once. If you just want to learn the basics then I hope I have always made it clear which they are and which are the more advanced concepts. The important thing is to go at the pace with which you are comfortable.

It is worth bearing in mind that every artificial convention you take on board has at least two ways in which it can cost you points. Firstly, it deprives you of the natural use of whatever bid is utilised in an artificial sense. Secondly, if either you or, more likely, partner forgets your agreement, disaster could follow. So only take on the more complex methods if you are happy that they are both a good idea and easy to remember.

Defensive bidding is a vital part of the game and you will be a far more successful player if you understand the methods and principles involved. And if you are like me, you enjoy winning.
May I wish you the best of luck.